Christmas Songs
FOR EASY GUITAR

ISBN 978-0-7935-1960-6

HAL•LEONARD®
CORPORATION

7777 W. BLUEMOUND RD. P.O. BOX 13819 MILWAUKEE, WI 53213

Visit Hal Leonard Online at
www.halleonard.com

Blue Christmas

Words and Music by Billy Hayes and Jay Johnson

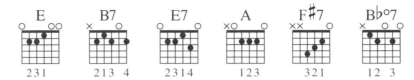

Verse

Moderate shuffle

1. I'll have a blue Christ-mas with-out you.
blue snow-flakes start fall-in',

I'll be so blue just think-ing a-bout you.
that's when the blue _____ mem-'ries start call-in'.

1.
Dec-o-ra-tions of red on a green Christ-mas
You'll be do-ing al-right with your

tree won't be the same, dear, if

2.
you're not here with me. 2. And when the Christ-mas of white, but

I'll have a blue, blue, blue, blue Christ-mas. _____

Merry Christmas, Darling

Words and Music by Richard Carpenter and Frank Pooler

Intro
Freely

Greet - ing cards have all been sent,

*Let chords ring throughout Intro

the Christ - mas rush is through, but I still have one

wish to make, a spe - cial one for you.

Verse
Moderately slow

Mer - ry Christ - mas, dar - ling. We're a - part, that's

true; but I can dream and in my dreams, I'm

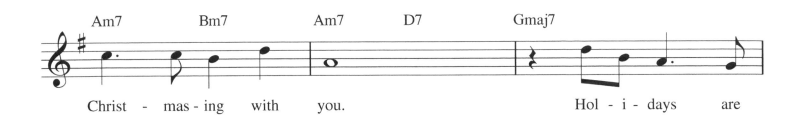

Christ - mas - ing with you. Hol - i - days are

joy - ful, there's al - ways some - thing new. But

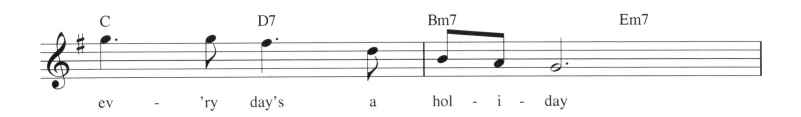

ev - 'ry day's a hol - i - day

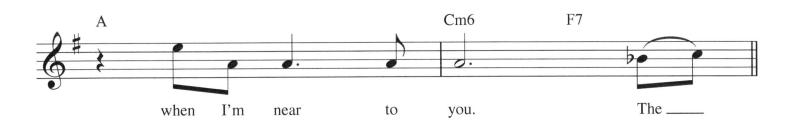

when I'm near to you. The _____

𝄋 Bridge

lights on my tree I wish you could see,

I wish it ev - 'ry day. The

The Christmas Song

(Chestnuts Roasting on an Open Fire)

Music and Lyrics by Mel Torme and Robert Wells

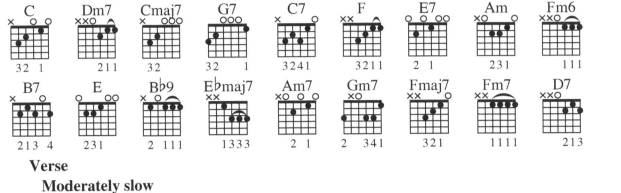

Verse

Moderately slow

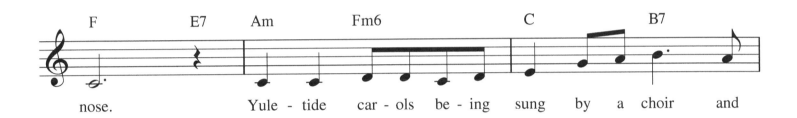

Chest-nuts roast-ing on an o-pen fire, Jack Frost nip-ping at your

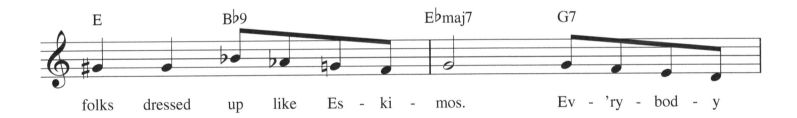

nose. Yule-tide car-ols be-ing sung by a choir and

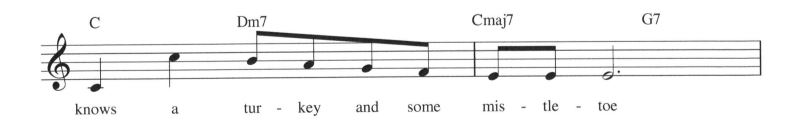

folks dressed up like Es-ki-mos. Ev-'ry-bod-y

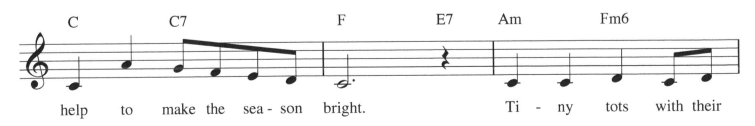

knows a tur-key and some mis-tle-toe

help to make the sea-son bright. Ti-ny tots with their

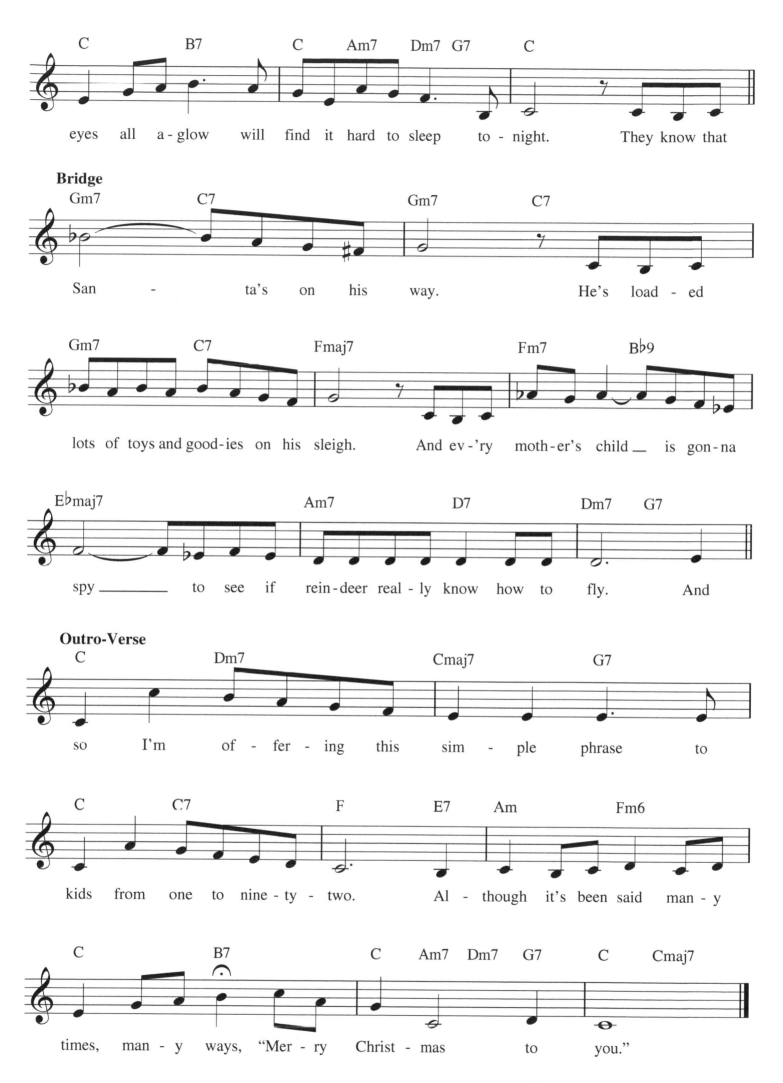

Christmas Time Is Here

from *A CHARLIE BROWN CHRISTMAS*

Words by Lee Mendelson
Music by Vince Guaraldi

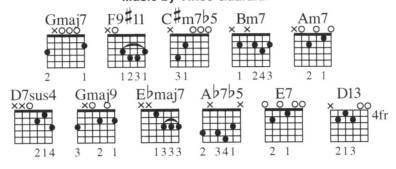

Verse
Slowly

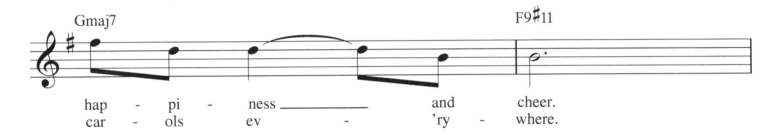

1. Christ - mas time _____ is here,
2. Snow - flakes in _____ the air,

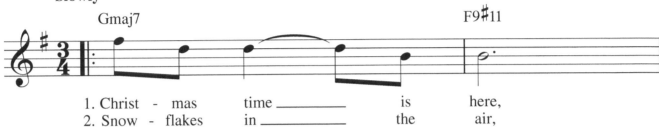

hap - pi - ness _____ and cheer.
car - ols ev - _____ 'ry - where.

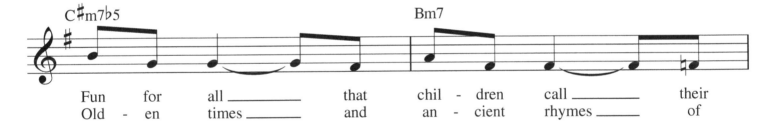

Fun for all _____ that chil - dren call _____ their
Old - en times _____ and an - cient rhymes _____ of

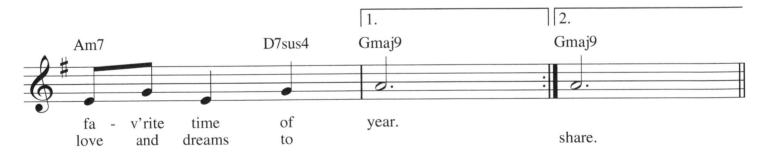

fa - v'rite time of year.
love and dreams to share.

Bridge

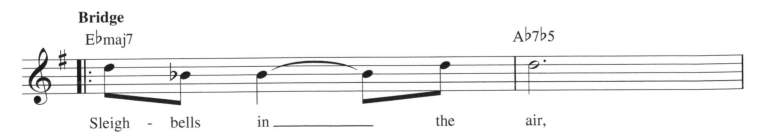

Sleigh - bells in _____ the air,

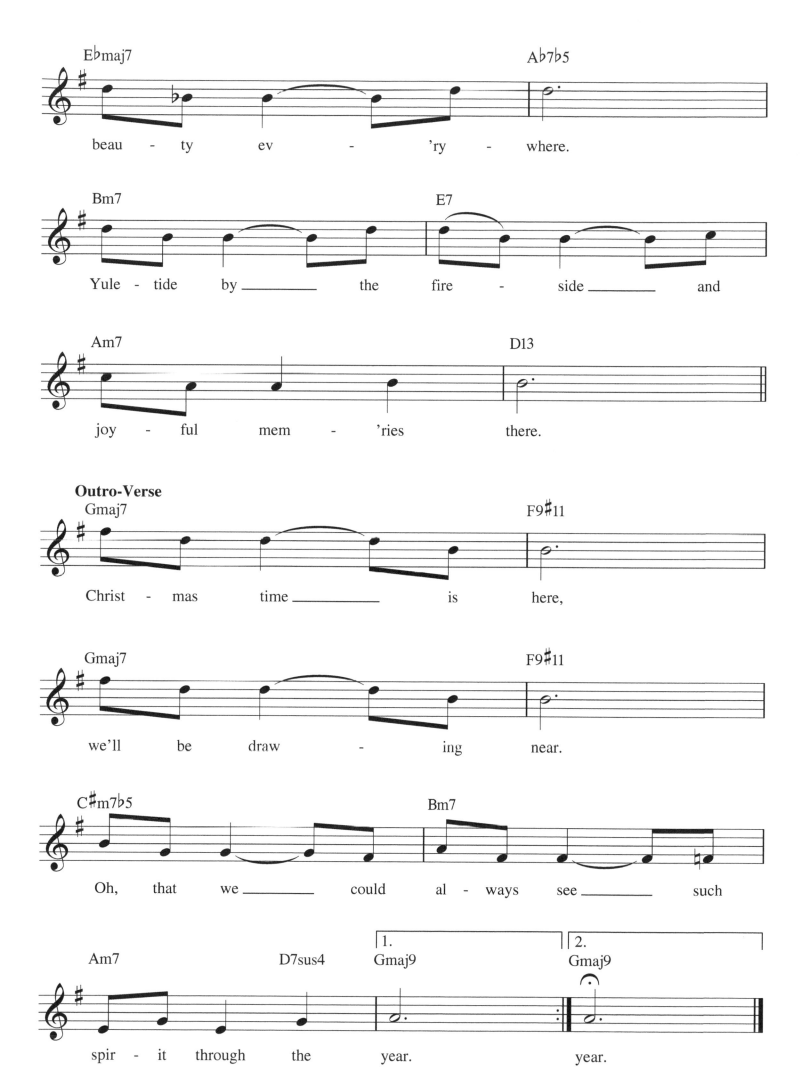

Do You Hear What I Hear

Words and Music by Noel Regney and Gloria Shayne

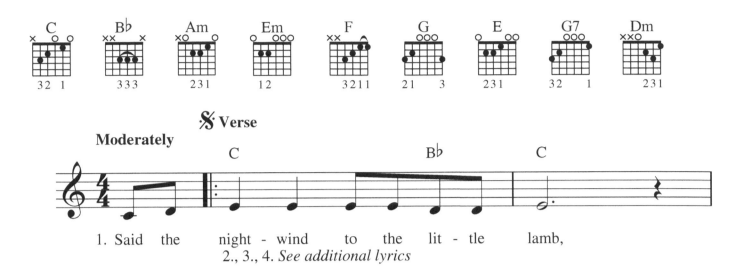

Moderately

% Verse

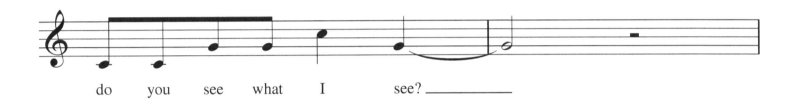

1. Said the night - wind to the lit - tle lamb,
2., 3., 4. *See additional lyrics*

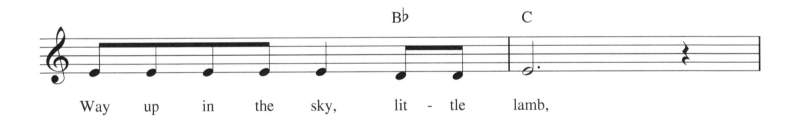

do you see what I see? _____

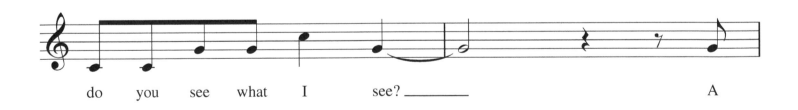

Way up in the sky, lit - tle lamb,

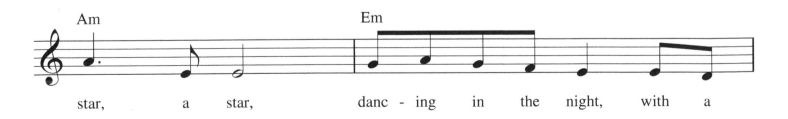

do you see what I see? _____ A

star, a star, danc - ing in the night, with a

tail   as   big   as   a   kite,   with   a   tail   as   big   as   a

kite.   2., 3. Said the   4. Said the

light,   He will bring   us   good - ness   and

light. _____

Additional Lyrics

2. Said the little lamb to the shepherd boy,
   Do you hear what I hear?
   Ringing through the sky, shepherd boy,
   Do you hear what I hear?
   A song, a song, high above the tree,
   With a voice as big as the sea,
   With a voice as big as the sea.

3. Said the shepherd boy to the mighty king,
   Do you know what I know?
   In your palace warm, mighty king,
   Do you know what I know?
   A Child, a Child shivers in the cold,
   Let us bring him silver and gold,
   Let us bring him silver and gold.

4. Said the king to the people ev'rywhere,
   Listen to what I say!
   Pray for peace, people ev'rywhere,
   Listen to what I say!
   The Child, the Child, sleeping in the night;
   He will bring us goodness and light,
   He will bring us goodness and light.

Frosty the Snow Man

Words and Music by Steve Nelson and Jack Rollins

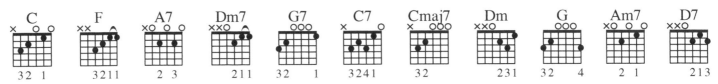

Verse
Moderately

1. Frost - y, the snow man was a jol - ly hap - py
3. Frost - y, the snow man knew the sun was hot that

soul, with a corn cob pipe and a but - ton nose and two
day, so he said, "Let's run and we'll have some fun now be -

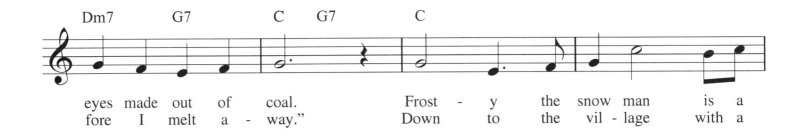

eyes made out of coal." Frost - y the snow man is a
fore I melt a - way." Down to the vil - lage with a

fair - y tale they say. He was made of snow but the chil - dren know how he
broom - stick in his hand, run - ning here and there, all a - round the square, say - in',

Bridge

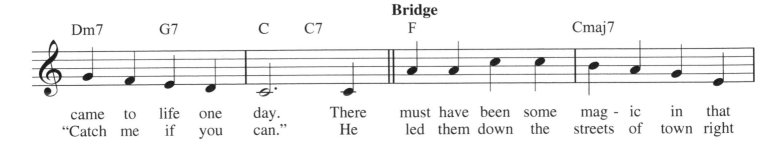

came to life one day. There must have been some mag - ic in that
"Catch me if you can." He led them down the streets of town right

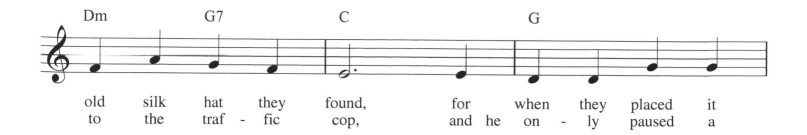

old   silk   hat   they   found,   for   when   they   placed   it
to   the   traf - fic   cop,   and   he   on - ly   paused   a

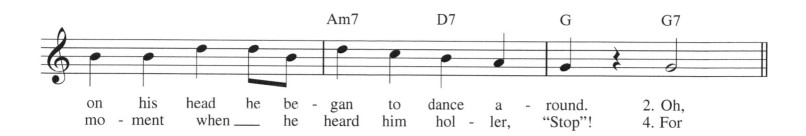

on   his   head   he   be - gan   to   dance   a - round.   2. Oh,
mo - ment   when ___ he   heard   him   hol - ler,   "Stop"!   4. For

Verse

Frost - y   the   snow man   was a - live   as   he   could   be,   and the
Frost - y   the   snow man   had to   hur - ry   on   his   way,   but he

chil - dren   say   he could   laugh and   play just the   same   as   you   and   me.
waved good - bye   say - in',   "Don't you   cry,   I'll be   back   a - gain some   day."

Outro

Thump - et - y   thump   thump, thump - et - y   thump   thump,   look   at   Frost - y   go.

Thump - et - y   thump   thump,   thump - et - y   thump   thump,   o - ver the hills of   snow.

Here Comes Santa Claus
(Right Down Santa Claus Lane)

Words and Music by Gene Autry and Oakley Haldeman

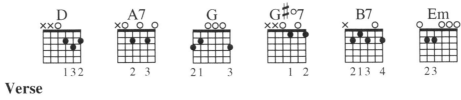

Verse
Moderately

1. Here comes San - ta Claus! Here comes San - ta Claus!
2., 3., 4. *See additional lyrics*

Right down San - ta Claus Lane!

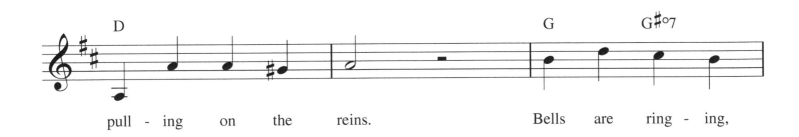

Vix - en and Blit - zen and all his rein - deer are

pull - ing on the reins.   Bells are ring - ing,

chil - dren sing - ing, all is mer - ry and

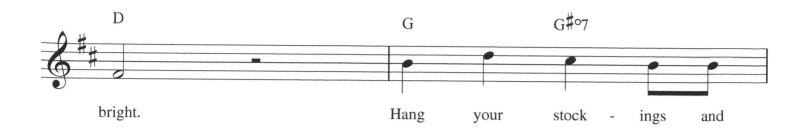

bright.   Hang   your   stock - ings   and

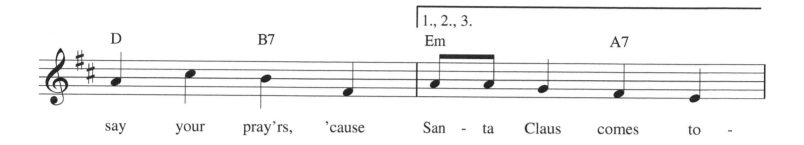

say   your   pray'rs, 'cause   San - ta   Claus   comes   to -

night.   San - ta   Claus   comes   to - night.

Additional Lyrics

2. Here comes Santa Claus! Here comes Santa Claus!
   Right down Santa Claus Lane!
   He's got a bag that is filled with toys
   For the boys and girls again.
   Here those sleigh bells jingle, jangle,
   What a beautiful sight.
   Jump in bed, cover up your head,
   Santa Claus comes tonight.

3. Here comes Santa Claus! Here comes Santa Claus!
   Right down Santa Claus Lane!
   He doesn't care if you're rich or poor,
   For he loves you just the same.
   Santa knows that we're God's children;
   That makes ev'rything right.
   Fill your hearts with a Christmas cheer,
   'Cause Santa Claus comes tonight.

4. Here comes Santa Claus! Here comes Santa Claus!
   Right down Santa Claus Lane!
   He'll come around when the chimes ring out;
   Then it's Christmas morn again.
   Peace on earth will come to all
   If we just follow the light.
   Let's give thanks to the Lord above,
   Santa Claus comes tonight.

A Holly Jolly Christmas

Music and Lyrics by Johnny Marks

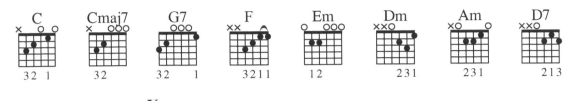

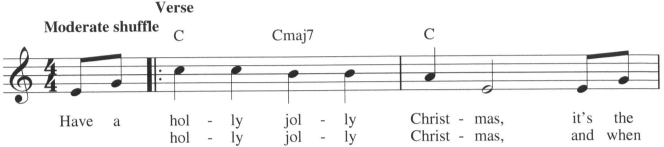

Verse
Moderate shuffle

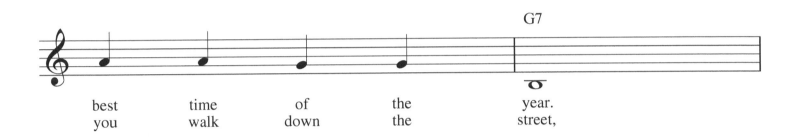

Have a hol - ly jol - ly Christ - mas, it's the
hol - ly jol - ly Christ - mas, and when

best time of the year.
you walk down the street,

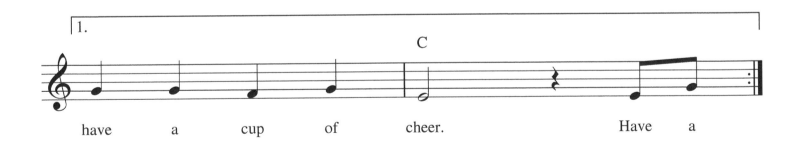

I don't know if there'll be snow but
say hel - lo to friends you know and

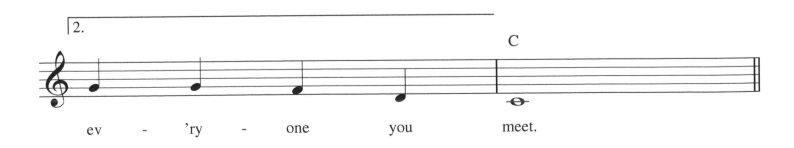

1.
have a cup of cheer. Have a

2.
ev - 'ry - one you meet.

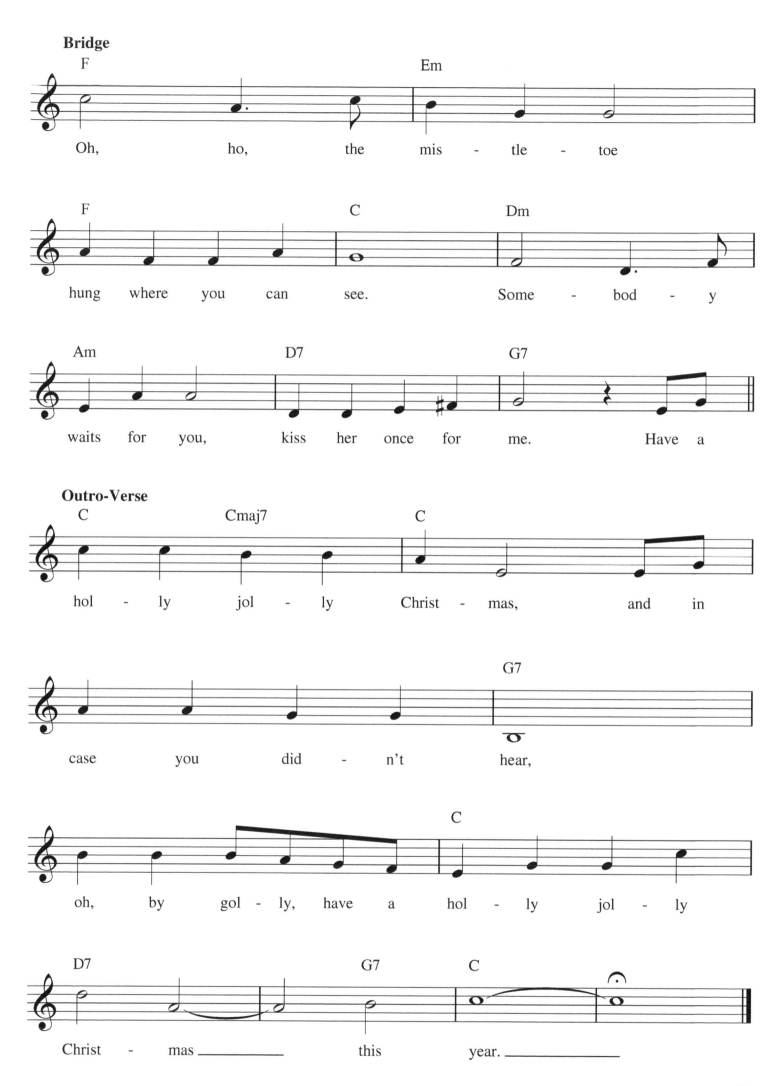

I Saw Mommy Kissing Santa Claus

Words and Music by Tommie Connor

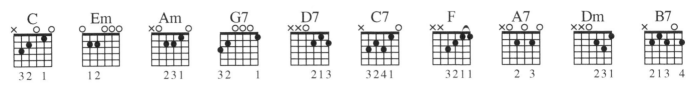

Verse
Moderately

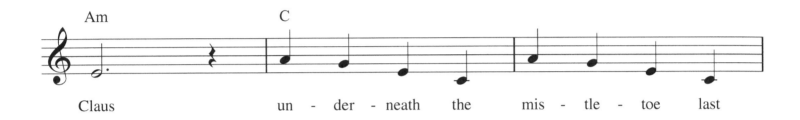

1., 2. I saw Mom - my kiss - ing San - ta

Claus un - der - neath the mis - tle - toe last

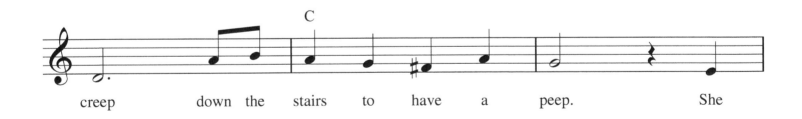

night. _____ She did - n't see me

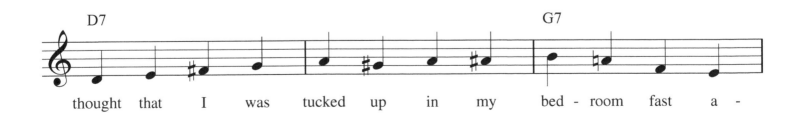

creep down the stairs to have a peep. She

D7   G7

thought that I was tucked up in my bed - room fast a -

sleep.   Then   I   saw   Mom - my   tick - le

San - ta   Claus   un - der - neath   his

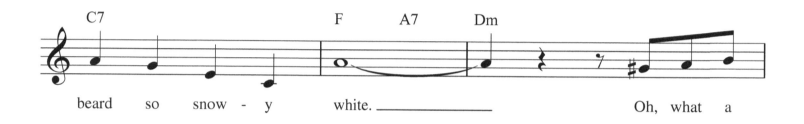

beard   so   snow - y   white. _____   Oh, what   a

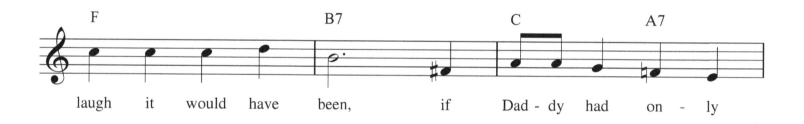

laugh   it   would   have   been,   if   Dad - dy   had   on - ly

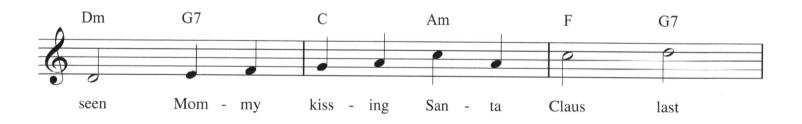

seen   Mom - my   kiss - ing   San - ta   Claus   last

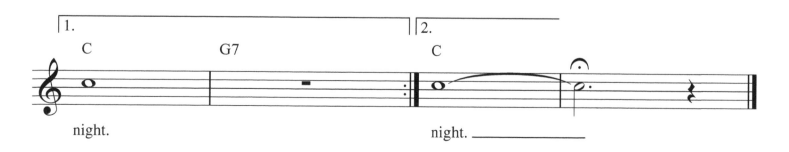

night.   night. _____

I'll Be Home for Christmas

Words and Music by Kim Gannon and Walter Kent

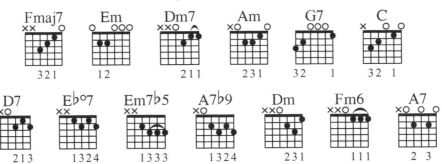

Intro
Moderately slow

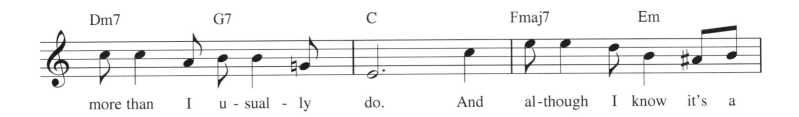

I'm dream-ing to-night of a place I love, e - ven

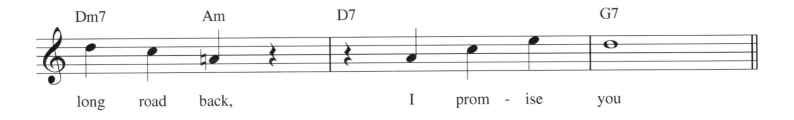

more than I u - sual - ly do. And al-though I know it's a

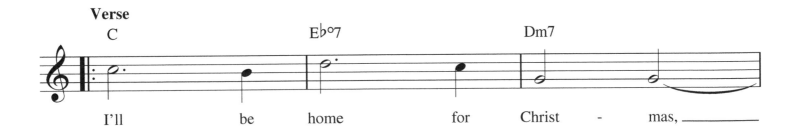

long road back, I prom - ise you

Verse

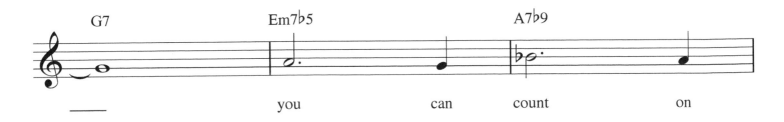

I'll be home for Christ - mas, _____ you can count on

me. _____ Please have snow and mis - tle - toe, and pre - sents on the tree. _____ Christ - mas Eve will find me _____ where the love - light gleams. _____ I'll be home for Christ - mas, if on - ly in my dreams. _____ dreams. _____

Jingle-Bell Rock

Words and Music by Joe Beal and Jim Boothe

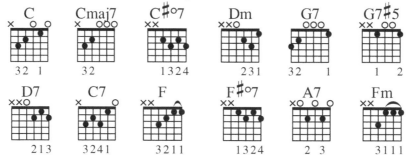

Verse
Moderate shuffle

Jin - gle - bell, jin - gle - bell, jin - gle - bell rock,
Jin - gle - bell, jin - gle - bell, jin - gle - bell rock,

jin - gle - bells swing and jin - gle - bells ring. Snow - in' and blow - in' up
jin - gle - bells chime in jin - gle - bell time. Dan - cin' and pran - cin' in

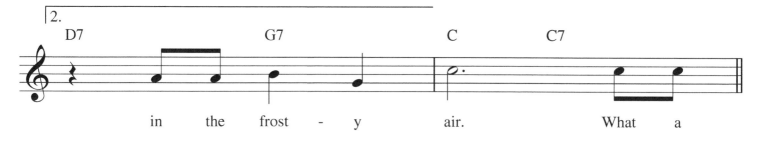

bush - els of fun, now the jin - gle - hop has be - gun. __
Jin - gle - bell Square

in the frost - y air. What a

Bridge

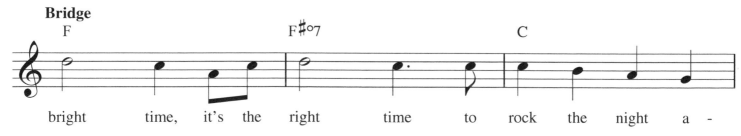

bright time, it's the right time to rock the night a -

way   Jin - gle - bell   time   is   a   swell   time

to   go   glid - in'   in   a   one   horse   sleigh.

Outro-Verse

Gid - dy - up,   jin - gle   horse   pick   up   your   feet,

jin - gle   a - round   the   clock.

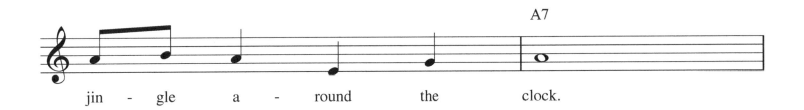

Mix   and   a   min - gle   in   the   jin - gle - in'   feet,

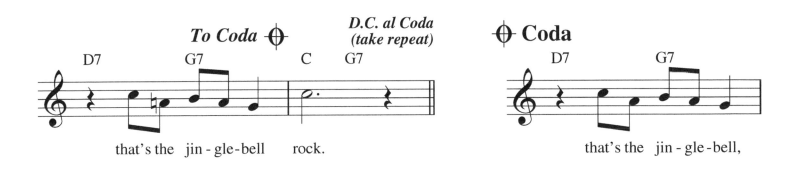

To Coda ⊕

D.C. al Coda
(take repeat)

⊕ **Coda**

that's the jin - gle-bell   rock.

that's the jin - gle - bell,

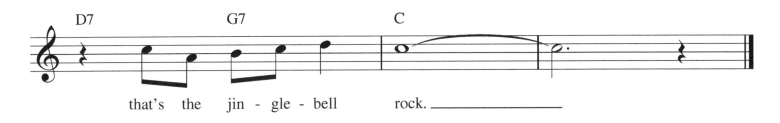

that's the jin - gle - bell   rock. _____

Let It Snow! Let It Snow! Let It Snow!

Words by Sammy Cahn
Music by Jule Styne

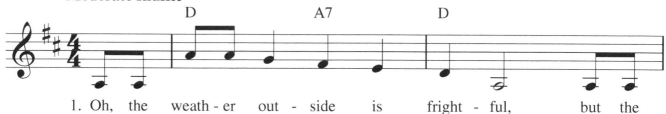

Verse
Moderate shuffle

1. Oh, the weath-er out-side is fright-ful, but the

fire is so de-light-ful. And

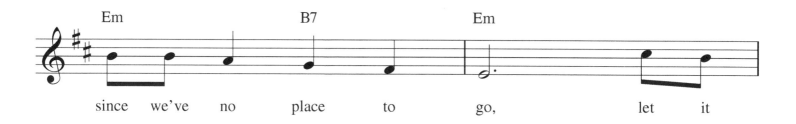

since we've no place to go, let it

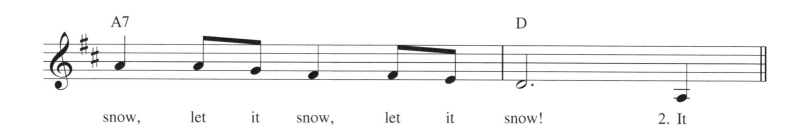

snow, let it snow, let it snow! 2. It

𝄋 Verse

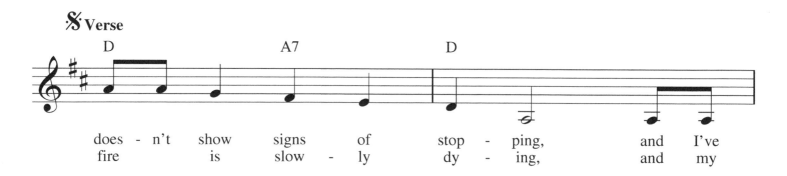

does-n't show signs of stop-ping, and I've
fire is slow-ly dy-ing, and my

A Marshmallow World

Words by Carl Sigman
Music by Peter De Rose

My Favorite Things

from THE SOUND OF MUSIC

Lyrics by Oscar Hammerstein II
Music by Richard Rodgers

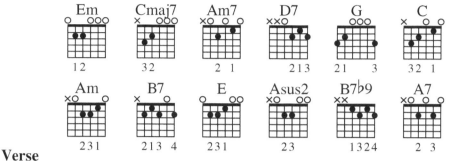

Verse
Moderately

1. Rain-drops on ros - es and whisk - ers on kit - tens,
2. Cream col - ored pon - ies and crisp ap - ple strud - els,

bright cop - per ket - tles and warm wool - en mit - tens;
door - bells and sleigh - bells and schnitz - el with noo - dles;

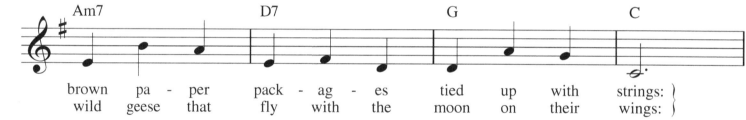

brown pa - per pack - ag - es tied up with strings:)
wild geese that fly with the moon on their wings:)

These are a few of my fa - vor - ite things.

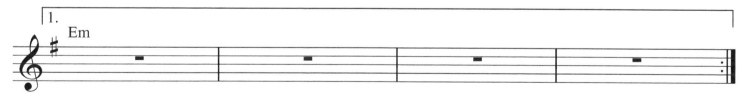

Verse

E

3. Girls in white dress - es with blue sat - in sash - es,

Asus2

snow - flakes that stay on my nose and eye - lash - es;

Am7   D7   G   C

sil - ver white win - ters that melt in - to springs:

G   C   Am   B7♭9

These are a few of my fa - vor - ite things.

Outro

Em   Am   B7   Em

When the dog bites, when the bee stings, when I'm feel - ing

C   A7

sad, _____ I sim - ply re - mem - ber my fa - vor - ite things and

G   C   D7   G

then I don't feel so bad. _____

C   G   D7   G

Rockin' Around the Christmas Tree

Music and Lyrics by Johnny Marks

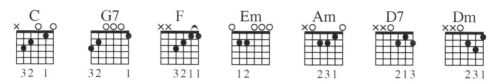

Verse

Moderate shuffle

Rock - in' a - round the Christ - mas tree ___ at the
Rock - in' a - round the Christ - mas tree, ___ let the

Christ - mas par - ty hop. ___ Mis - tle - toe hung where
Christ - mas spir - it ring. ___ Lat - er we'll have some

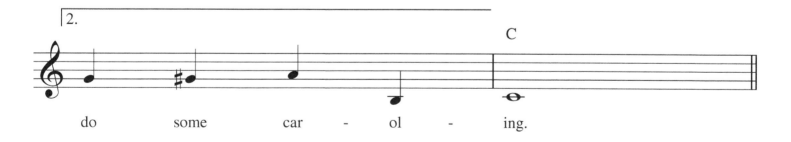

you can see ___ ev - 'ry cou - ple tries to stop.
pump - kin pie ___ and we'll

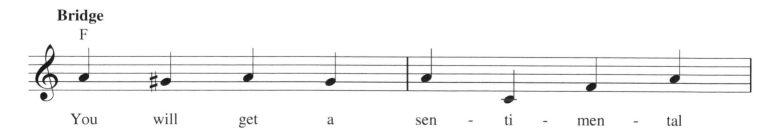

do some car - ol - ing.

Bridge

You will get a sen - ti - men - tal

Rudolph the Red-Nosed Reindeer

Music and Lyrics by Johnny Marks

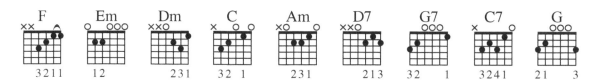

Intro
Freely

You know Dash - er and Danc - er and Pranc - er and Vix - en,

Com - et and Cu - pid and Don - ner and Blitz - en, but do you re -

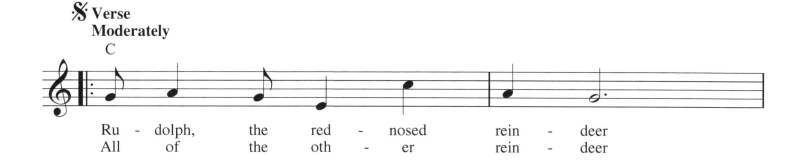

call the most fa - mous rein - deer of all?

Verse
Moderately

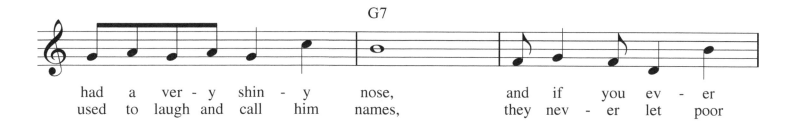

Ru - dolph, the red - nosed rein - deer
All of the oth - er rein - deer

had a ver - y shin - y nose, and if you ev - er
used to laugh and call him names, they nev - er let poor

Silver Bells

from the Paramount Picture THE LEMON DROP KID
Words and Music by Jay Livingston and Ray Evans

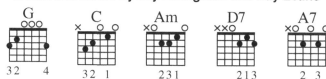

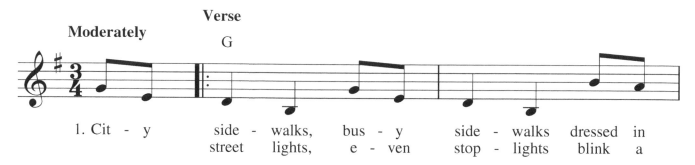

Verse

Moderately

1. Cit - y side - walks, bus - y side - walks dressed in
street lights, e - ven stop - lights blink a

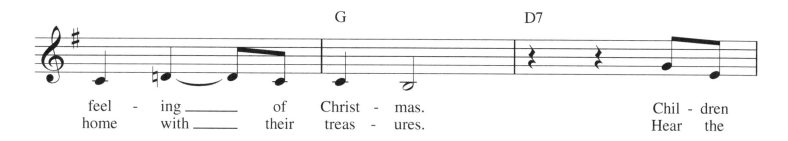

hol - i - day style, in the air there's a
bright red and green, as the shop - pers rush

feel - ing _____ of Christ - mas.   Chil - dren
home with _____ their treas - ures.   Hear the

laugh - ing, peo - ple pass - ing, meet - ing smile af - ter
snow crunch, see the kids bunch, this is San - ta's big

smile,   and on ev - 'ry street cor - ner you'll
scene,   and a - bove all this bus - tle you'll

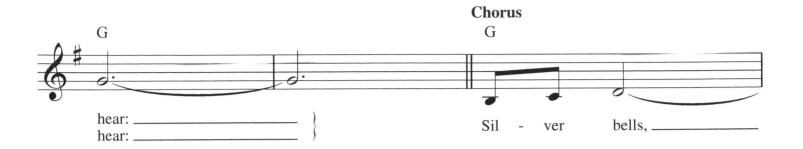

Chorus

Silver bells, _____

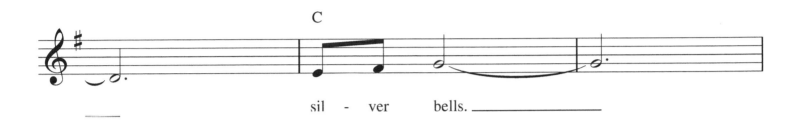

sil - ver bells. _____

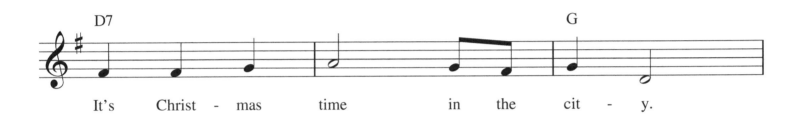

It's Christ - mas time in the cit - y.

Ring - a - ling, _____ hear them ring. _____

Soon it will be Christ - mas

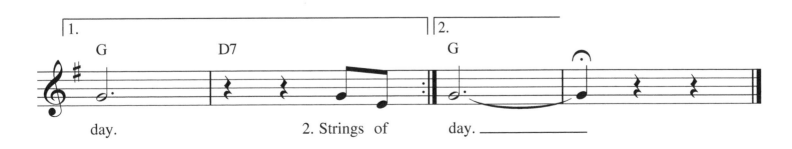

1.
day.   2. Strings of
2.
day. _____

Suzy Snowflake

Words and Music by Sid Tepper and Roy Bennett

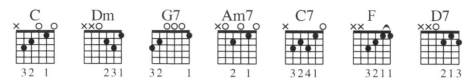

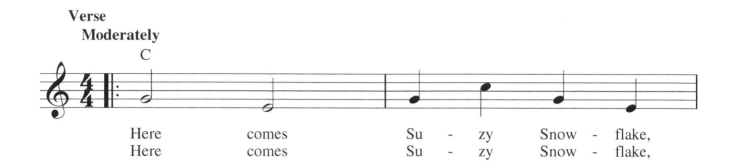

Verse
Moderately

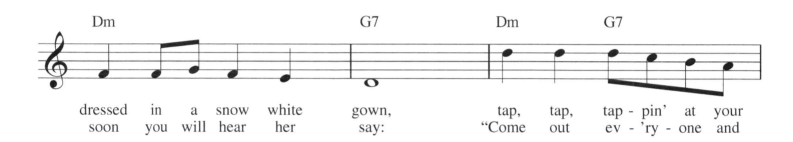

Here comes Su- zy Snow- flake,
Here comes Su- zy Snow- flake,

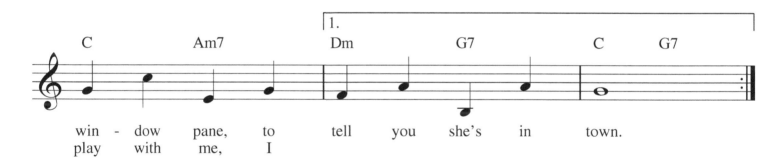

dressed in a snow white gown, tap, tap, tap- pin' at your
soon you will hear her say: "Come out ev- 'ry- one and

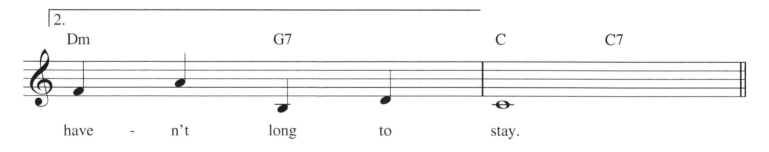

1.
win- dow pane, to tell you she's in town.
play with me, I

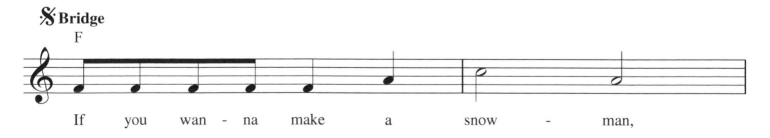

2.
have- n't long to stay.

%Bridge

If you wan- na make a snow- man,

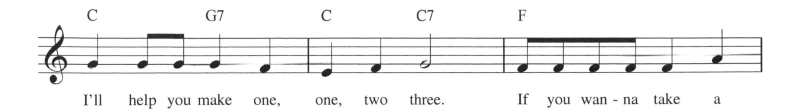

I'll help you make one, one, two three. If you wan-na take a

sleigh ride, the ride's on me."

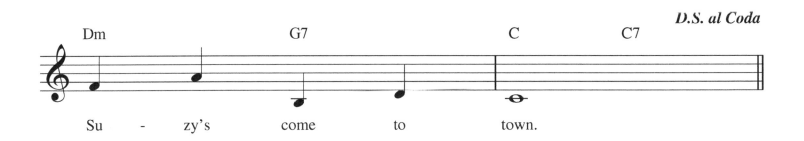

Outro-Verse

Here comes Su-zy Snow-flake, look at her tum-blin'

To Coda ⊕

down. Bring-ing joy to ev-'ry girl and boy,

D.S. al Coda

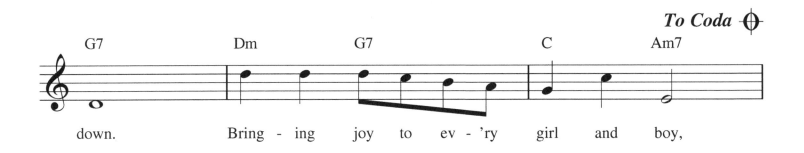

Su-zy's come to town.

⊕ **Coda**

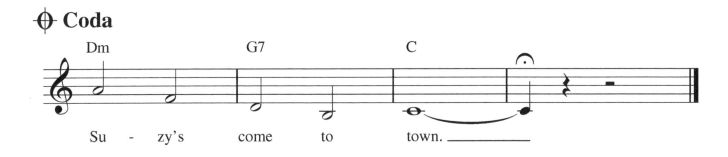

Su-zy's come to town.____

You're All I Want for Christmas

Words and Music by Glen Moore and Seger Ellis

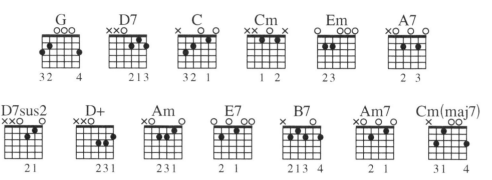

Intro
Dreamily

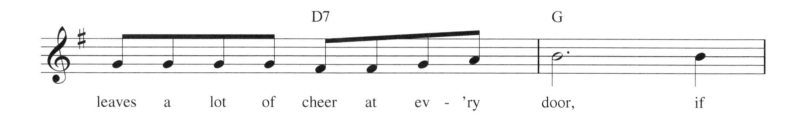

When San - ta comes a - round at Christ - mas time and

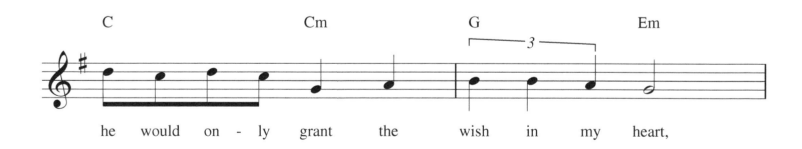

leaves a lot of cheer at ev - 'ry door, if

C   Cm   G   Em

he would on - ly grant the wish in my heart,

I would nev - er ask for more You're

Santa Claus Is Comin' to Town

Words by Haven Gillespie
Music by J. Fred Coots